UNTETHERED

LIVING AND LEADING LIBERATION

Leadership Memoir

LESLIE AYORKOR EDWARDS

Printed in the United States

To protect identity, some names have been changed.

Published by EdLeadership4Liberation

Editing and graphic design by Karen Bowlding

Cover image by: paylessimages

ISBN: 979-8-218-25149-9

Library of Congress Control Number: 2023914479

Printed in the United States

Dedication

This book is dedicated to my family, who have relentlessly supported me, buoyed me with fervent prayers, and kept me rooted in God and His promises over my life.

-

To countless friends and colleagues who have shared encouraging words at the precise moments when I most needed them as well as inspired me to hold fast to my dreams and purpose.

-

To my beautiful friend Melissa, who gained her wings entirely too soon, but blessed me with the gift of embracing my journey and all of life's lessons along the way.

-

And last, but certainly not least, my children who fuel my commitment to show up as the best version of myself and leave a legacy that honors my faith and my ancestors. Thank you all for helping me liberate myself!

Acknowledgements

Writing this book has truly been a process of healing and affirmation. I am grateful. I am blessed. And I am liberated! This could not have been possible without my Lord and Savior: Thank you Lord for helping me to give myself permission to speak my truth. I am forever indebted to my ancestors, fellow educators, and countless leaders that have helped to shape my testimony and my truth.

Prologue

Welcome to my undoing. My untethered odyssey toward a new North Star: living and leading liberation. This leadership memoir begins with unraveling the layers of my personal life that led to a greater self-awareness and an increased alignment with my purpose, peace, and passion for educational leadership. This reading experience is for anyone that is seeking healing and harmony as they navigate life, bridging leadership theory, and personal manifestation in a manner that hasn't been done. Let's not just change *how* we tell our stories, let's shift the compass of our narratives altogether!

My story is raw as I unpack experiences that I haven't allowed to escape my lips until now, namely confronting the fact that I ran from the reality of losing my virginity by being raped at a high school party and subsequently processed my rape as a rite of passage for finally being acknowledged as something other than being the Black girl in a predominantly all-white suburban school. Unbeknownst to me, that experience, along with many others I touched on in this leadership memoir, had a direct impact on how I showed up as a leader in my personal life and in my career as an educator.

If you have ever felt the realities of what you hoped a certain experience, job, or even a person would be, just to witness everything crumble around you into a million shards of broken mirrors that force you to see the countless reflections of yourself, then you are in the right place and in good company.

The definition of the word "untethered" is unbound, unrestrained, not tied or limited in any fashion. Not being compelled to use this word in conversation or in writing until now, the title simply rolled off of my tongue well after starting to write what I initially thought would be a free-write journal to help me unpack a crossroad I was facing as a woman, wife, mother, and educational leader.

Generally, when I heard people refer to themselves as being at a crossroad, I imagined it as a distinct moment when someone was at the precipice of a decision or milestone. However, as you will see throughout this memoir, my journey toward personal and professional liberation has been an avalanche of several years that is still evolving today. The culmination of my avalanche toppled down on me when I least expected it and became a relentless visitor in the middle of the night, an unset alarm clock determined to disrupt the slumber-state of consciousness I had accepted for myself. My awakening signal started as a deep, guttural feeling that began, like a whisper, to get up. However, soon after, it turned into an uncompromising knot in my throat followed by a military bugle wake up call. And with my awakening came an accompaniment of deafening screams from my ancestors.

It was as though they were calling me out of my internal hiding place, conjuring a spirit of self-assurance within me that I regrettably abandoned to manufacture truths from the lies that had once sustained me; lies that set up real estate in my mind and forced me to reflect on the historic hardships my ancestors experienced as slaves. However, my ancestors were stirring up a revived narrative in my spirit to reinforce that they had not only used the spices from the earth to create our original remedies, they engrained healing in our ancestral DNA. My ancestors had not only built pyramids with the most complex mathematics to date, they constructed unbreakable resilience and intellect within our people. They were the original astronomers, deciphering the constellations in the sky that allowed the heavenlies to illuminate their path to freedom. My ancestors were not only picking cotton, they were also sowing the seeds that I am reaping today. They shaped my pedigree for liberation. I am my ancestors, and they are me.

My liberation helped me to center on the misnomer of the Atlantic Slave Trade kidnapping slaves. When in reality, slavers stole the bodies of healers, doctors, mothers and fathers, mathematicians, educators, scientists. They were my ancestors, kidnapped from their homeland and dehumanized to the unimaginable labor of picking cotton from sunup to sundown, void of remittance. Cotton is known as being a durable and highly absorbent fabric. It is used to source essential items such as clothing, undergarments, bedding, and even jackets. In fact, cotton is the first plant that was able to germinate on the moon! How ironic that, on the backs of my ancestors, textiles every human being needs to survive cost them their freedom.

My spiritual revival elevated a deep gratitude for my ancestors as true life givers. Because of them, I am the woman, mother, sister, friend, educator, and leader I am today. I am durable cotton, a tapestry of fabrics woven from inventors, builders, astronomers, herbalists, and peacekeepers. I am life-giving garments, embellished with hope for an unforeseen future. I am my liberated ancestors.

Thank you for joining my unchartered journey as an author, an authentic illustration of how I found myself misaligned with my purpose in my personal life as well as my role as an educational leader. Our journey together will be interactive. You will have the opportunity to reflect on various questions I peppered throughout your reading experience. I urge you to be an active participant as you navigate what liberation looks like for you to confront how you show up as a leader in your family, friendships, church, and/or professional life. For this reading journey, let's rip off the self-imposed band-aid laced with societal expectations and mental trenches. Let's just be untethered together on this journey. Unbound by labels and judgment, truly liberated. Let's get started!

Contents

chapter one

Untethered by Taking Childhood Ashes to Burn Sage

In 2017, the phrase "Black Girl Magic" seemed to float on the wave of the poise and self-assuredness of our eternal FLOTUS, Michelle Obama. Being the first African American first lady of the United States, Michelle Obama embodied a wonderful tapestry of ancestral strength. When watching news coverage of her at schools surrounded by children, one couldn't deny her sweet spirit. This spirit seemed to derive from our late Queen Nzinga who ruled the Ndongo and Matamba Kingdoms. Her spirit of triumph, of overcoming political obstacles, and creating a narrative of resilience that so many of us fall victim to, were all woven together into an Afrocentric dreadlock. In fact, legend has it that Queen Nzinga was born with the umbilical cord wrapped around her neck, nearly dying at birth, but a wise woman in the room quickly untethered her from the cord, thus saving her life.

Oh, the strongholds we escape just to find ourselves in entanglements all the same.

The steady conflict I faced for the last several years was the dance between that archetype of a woman. The graceful, sweeping leaps of a poised ballet dancer perfecting my pirouette to sacrifice self for family and career duties was beginning to hear a new melodic rhythm of steel drums that only syncopated pelvic thrusts and a swinging waist could tame. You see, the internal conflict I experienced for several years was, in part, driven by a new generation of women taking up a different baton of the female archetype. Women from all walks of life were starting to paint outside of the lines, re-defining womanhood and embracing the road not taken. A new climate of femininity emerged with the courage of Malala Yousafzai, fighting for the education of women across the globe, CaShawn Thompson, a native Washingtonian and mother of two, who fueled a new energy of women's empowerment with her Black Girl Magic hashtag, Glennon Doyle who helped to build community rooted in the shared experiences to disrupt the limited perceptions of womanhood, and Alexandria Ocasio-Cortez, referred to as AOC, whose political activism let the world know that women won't be silenced.

An existential sisterhood began to form at the center of a new universe with constellations like Issa Rae, who reminded us that the brilliance of our shine is in our authenticity, Viola Davis whose intergalactic energy made us all shine brighter, the celestial glow of Chimamanda Ngozi Adichie expressed to us we have a voice and story that matters, the bombastic and revelatory charge from Iyanla Vanzant to fix our lives, and the eternal radiance of everything Oprah represents as our ancestor's wildest dreams, emblazoned a new sense of pride across the globe, especially amongst women of color. The fire was ignited across social media and in the homes of many of us, who, possibly like me, were initially intrigued by the glow from this blaze for our daughters. Every time I found myself feeling inspired by another woman of color, I immediately thought of a way to pour the revelation into my daughter, Anaya.

However, this radical revolution was suddenly beginning to take on a new life within my own journey as a woman, wife, mother, and educational leader. For the first time, I started interrogating my discontented tears and unearthing the roots of my proverbial weeping willow. Why was I allowing myself to feel so confined? Why did I feel tethered to only coloring within the lines and arriving at decisions to make others feel comfortable? Could two things be true at the same time? Was I overthinking everything? Why couldn't I be assertive about things that mattered to me and pursue my passions, while being committed to my family and career as an educator? The storm of questions swirling in my mind began to signal a shift in my forecast.

I arrived at a foreboding mental intersection and could no longer hide from myself. My newfound Black Girl Magic and the platform I had as a Black woman leader, serving hundreds of other school leaders, had me choking on the possibility of what could be. Seeing traction from the He For She Movement with men like Matt Damon using his platform to advocate for access to sanitation for women, John Legend calling men to become feminists in a way that hadn't been done, and Tyler Perry putting the faces of countless women that looked like me in leading roles, all signaled to me that my evolution as a women was shifting, and it was time for me to accept the invitation toward liberation. The whispers of my ancestors turned into a resounding call of strength and fortitude. And so, my journey to discover self and explore the process of untethering from the fallacies of the archetypal cinder blocks that weigh on women across the globe began.

Before you begin cheering for the genesis of my untethered journey, let me position myself with humility and vulnerability. Black Girl Magic was the antithesis of my austere persona growing up. As a child, I felt like my skin betrayed me and hung like a dilapidated curtain over the stained-glass windows of my soul. Because I attended schools with predominantly white children, educators, and neighbors, I didn't see myself reflected in those around me, and sadly enough, I didn't see myself in my own reflection in the mirror. The comments from boys at school with whom I had crushes on swirled in my head each time I looked in the mirror: "Leslie's pretty for a Black girl. Leslie's cool, but my family would never let me date a Black girl!" Those racially charged comments became melodies in mind, and like a broken record player, robbed me of escaping the monotony of not being good enough to be truly seen by others; sometimes not even being seen by my own self.

As my vulnerability nags on me as I write, I'm buckling a belted memory I've not spoken aloud to my closest friends, which is centered on my unhealthy relationship with the concept of feeling seen. They say healing only begins to happen when you speak truth to power. My truth is that when I was 15 years old, I processed my rape by a white upperclassman with the notion of finally being seen beyond the chocolate chip in a sea of milk. Being a rape victim wasn't a title I accepted nor something I openly spoke about. Even today, I feel a sense of detachment from my experience. However, those fraught words that congested my voice box for decades now serve as a balm to my continued healing.

Like liberation, healing doesn't have one destination, but instead journeys like a nomad within your soul and subconscious, looking for a new home to delight in. And so, I openly submit to what it looks like to process being raped decades after it occurred. My rapist, who I will call A.L., was one of the boys who shared those vain expressions of me being pretty...for a black girl. And like many Black teenage girls in schools with few people of color, my desire to fit in and momentarily feel like "Becky with the good hair" battled with my tightly coiled African roots I so keenly attempted to hot comb each morning.

On one particular evening, A.L. was throwing a house party, and to my freshman mentality, attending a senior party was fertile ground for being seen. Exploiting the night well beyond what my girlfriends and I could handle, after several shots of alcohol, we were passed out in the hallway of the second floor of A.L's home. I was picked up by someone and tossed on top of a bed. Between inebriated confusion, I realized that A.L was raping me while simultaneously pinning my arms down and whispering in my ear to be quiet. And so, I did. What A.L. didn't know was that he was shoplifting my virginity as his prized possession. While being a virgin wasn't the popular thing in high school, it was something I knew would be worth securing until my love story I naively watched in movies like *Dirty Dancing* became my reality. In that moment, when I allowed A.L. to silence me, it sunk into my spirit as a veil I wore well into adulthood. That night, I learned to sell muted promises and hushed dreams to myself; not truly liberating myself to speak my truth.

The thief of my virginity didn't know I was struggling with wanting to feel seen, and in that moment, A.L. sounded a deeper alarm that aroused my conundrum of what it truly meant to be seen and heard for my authentic self. Once he fell asleep, I was quiet as I tiptoed out of his bedroom. Days after the party, when school resumed, I shamefully glanced at A.L. while passing in the hallway. He shot a mild grin at me.

An undignified voice in my head said, "You see? It wasn't that bad. At least he knows you exist now."

That same undignified voice followed me beyond the brick and mortar of the schoolhouse and into my adulthood. Whenever I became afraid that revealing a truth could hurt someone else, or even worse, afraid of the truths that could awaken the scabs of my own hurt, I began to operate in my newly acquired vow of silence.

Take a moment and reflect on a singular truth about your past or present you are scared to face. While your truth doesn't define you, it plays an important role in shaping your own story into your song. Using your ashes to burn sage begins with facing those truths. Even if they are just your truths, they matter and deserve to be seen and heard by you and others whenever you're ready.

Like a cavern that needs to be unearthed, unpacking your truth gives you the opportunity to heal the layers that made you who you are. Caverns are a natural void in the ground shaped by weathering rock. They are only as majestic as the jagged sediments that create mesmerizing formations. Your truths hang from the caverns of your soul waiting to be discovered by tourists that seek to encounter an awakening from what lies beneath. Do the work. Welcome tourists into your caverns. Let the rocks fall where they may. Use your ashes to burn sage!

Some people might say I shouldn't have gone to the party and participated in under-age drinking. Had I been home in bed that night, I wouldn't have been raped. However, my truth is: I was a teenager learning about life, making some bad decisions, but I didn't give consent and therefore didn't deserve to be raped. While it is part of the tourist stops in my cavern, it doesn't define the worth of my tourist attraction.

It was not until decades later that I began to snatch my healing from A.L. while on a trip to Ghana, attending a tour of the Cape Coast Castle. When I arrived at the castle, I immediately saw the towering white citadel, akin to an ivory chateau with palatial windows and grandiose door designs, carved from the most luxurious wood etchings, juxtaposed with the canons that lined its ocean shores. Canons, which housed the secrets of bloodshed, tears, and molested transgressions, blasted out generations that couldn't keep the secrets of systemic oppression and broken promises of colorblindness.

Cape Coast Castle is the fortress where my ancestors were chained, beaten, and treated like cattle, crowded into the tunnels of the belly of the castle as ships, manned by slavers that filled the shoreline with the intentions of kidnapping the culture, hopes, and bodies of my people.

As the tour guide began to recall the events that actualized from those intentions, he described the conditions my ancestors endured, namely elevating that slave capturers took a liking to young virgins, and oftentimes, the younger African women were raped by white slavers in the cramped rooms, while the shackles remained adorned on their limbs.

As I walked through the bowels of Cape Coast Castle, my memory of A.L. sprung like vomit from my belly into the ducts of my eyes and flooded the castle like a ravenous tsunami obliterating everything in its way. Have you ever had a moment when you wept for the person you were during a life altering event, well after morphing into an entirely different person altogether? I thought I was no longer the young girl at the high school party, but in that moment, the teenage girl surfaced within me. To the other people on the tour, I'm sure they imagined my tears were solely about the conditions slaves endured. My tears were for the battered wrists and ankles from the iron chains that pinned my ancestors as they were raped, just like 15-year-old me with A.L.'s pale hands holding me down.

In that moment, the spirit of my ancestors was alive in me more than ever before. It wasn't as if I was unaware of the fact that slaves were brutally raped by their overseers for sport. Through my own personal studies of the dynamics of slave plantations, I was keenly cognizant of the historical molestation of slaves, both male and female. However, there was something about hearing it being said while in actual slave quarters in Ghana that uncorked my bottle of tears I hadn't cried about my rape. Wrapped in a maze of emotions, I wept for my ancestors who couldn't cry out as they languished on the cold, concrete floors of the castle. And I cried for myself, still being held captive to false limitations guiding my blind pilgrimage toward increased harmony in my life.

It wasn't until my return from my trip to Ghana that I sought out therapy to begin to unpack the bondage of my younger self. And as I began working on myself, further reflections revealed the implications of those tears in Ghana on how I show up as a leader. At that time, I was a new school leader and needed to unpack my adolescent boxes of imposter syndrome, stemming from wanting to feel seen and heard throughout my teenage years.

And as we all know, when we start unpacking boxes, we are bound to find some things we are grateful we packed to bring to a new place of residence, and other things we realize shouldn't have made it into the box in the first place. The learning is in the fact that the power lies in us realizing we have the choice to decide whether to keep the item or toss it into a separate box bound for donations. It forces us to contemplate the time when the item was actually of value to us, and we wouldn't have considered tossing it away. However, the newer version of us no longer has the attachment to the item and wishes to exchange it as collateral for cleansing our mind to create space for something new to serve the person we are in the present. In essence, giving up collateral is like burning sage for your life, clearing out energies and perspectives that create a distorted version of yourself.

Now, stay with me on the collateral metaphor because in leadership, I like to call this unpacking process, the Collateral Damage Box. At some point in our lives, we allowed someone to borrow something in exchange for collateral that we held onto until the original item was returned. In fact, you may have been the student who often borrowed a pencil from your teacher and used your favorite crayon box or prized bookbag as collateral. The key is that the collateral had to be something of value to make the exchange equitable. The same is true with interactions as a leader: Equitable relationships with the people you lead are rooted in honoring and affirming something of value they possess in order to avoid accruing collateral damage.

Similar to how I believed that my skin wasn't honored and affirmed as a student, I later missed opportunities to speak up, minimized myself in professional settings, and felt like the token Black person who had to represent the entire race, I consciously and subconsciously accrued collateral damage as a leader.

Your collateral box is made up of what you value and hold in high regard. And as a leader, what you value drives your decisions, the narrative in your mind, and how you build and nurture relationships. Whatever our leadership role, we all lead from our present seat. Whether it's in your family, church, school, and/or organization, the contents of your Leadership Collateral Box are the things that promote your purpose and healing or pin and silence you. Reflecting on this chapter, take a moment to conduct an inventory of your Leadership Collateral Box. Lean into a revelation that is holding your leadership potential captive and give it voice, action, and permission to no longer create collateral damage in your life and in your role as a leader.

Use the following questions to remove items from your Leadership Collateral Box to fuel your liberation:

What was one life changing event you experienced that proved you are stronger than you realized?

____

____

____

____

____

Symbolically remove this item or memory from your box and take your strength with you to drive your continued liberation and to inspire others!

When was a time in your life you felt silenced by the gravity of a situation or by the actions of someone else?

____

____

____

____

____

Take a moment to speak your truth aloud or call someone you trust and is judgment free. Express your truth and commitment to no longer being silenced by anyone or anything. Remove your voice from your box. You will need your power to speak your truth as you continue to liberate yourself and others.

What is a limitation you are placing on yourself due to fear or another emotion preventing you from being your authentic self? Where does that emotion come from?

____

____

____

____

____

Unearthing the roots of your fears will support your ability to sustain a liberated mindset. Take a moment and think about the things you value and have given up for collateral for something far less valuable. Push yourself to think through why you give up values such as peace, boundaries, travel, high standards, and liberation for barren promises and sterile titles. Place your fears in your box and remove your self-worth and personal values. You will need them along your liberation journey. Now let's seal your box with items that no longer serve you during your journey and ship it without a return label!

chapter two

Untethered by Knowing Your Leadership Birthright

I come from a lineage of women that endured being ripped from their families and native homes, incessantly raped by their oppressors, and awakened before the rising of the sun to work in the field, impregnated with lost dreams and decimated traditions. I come from "Wade, in the water...Wade, in the water children...Wade, in the water. God's gonna trouble the water!" I come from babies wrapped like the most anticipated Christmas gifts with kente cloth on the backs of women with sun-kissed African skin. I come from majestic pyramids tall enough to slap the heavens and make the clouds jealous. I come from mines buttressed with gold and diamonds—the true jewels of the Nile.

As an African woman, wealth, willpower, and wisdom are my birthright. However, at a crossroad in my life, all I could muster was a sense of weariness. I began to lose my sense of resolve, and in fact, grew to resent the use of the word "resilience." I was struggling to manage my role as a mother of two, wife, school leader, not to mention, an owner of a single-family style home no longer maintaining the air of cleanliness I once coveted. Most people may call my accomplishments a blessing. I dreamt of this life as a child, only to be drowning in it all. At a point in my life, I wasn't connected to my ancestral strength or any archetype of a woman for that matter. I felt emotionally barren and angry about the fixed path I felt lay before me.

I loved my children immensely but felt they extinguished the dreamer in me. Living up to the expectations I believed my husband had for me, left me with a daily reminder of my shortcomings. The students, staff, and parents at the school I led required so much of me. I had to abandon any remaining self-indulges. Every emotion I experienced was connected to my service to others. I no longer gave myself permission to enjoy only what benefited me. My ambitions to balance a leadership career in education as a wife and mother were replaced with incomplete to-do lists, continual commutes to keep up with the kid's activities, and unactuated promises to slow down and make time for self-care. Whether the voice is a whisper from the cavity of lack in your throat, a cry of lies your gut has fed you to believe, or a heightened scream from the denials you've trained your heart to make excuses for, these voices make you begin to doubt everything you know to be true about your personal fortitude as a person and as a leader.

Your resolute, "I can do this!" gets replaced with, "Can I do this?" and "At what cost am I pushing through this?" In these moments, I sometimes wondered how ancestors like Sojourner Truth and Harriet Tubman squelched the persistent voices of defeat in the midst of the screaming wars within. Did they make deals with the devil, secretly abandoning overwhelmed precipices for self-deprecating lofts that satisfied short-lived personal hopes and dreams? Did they ever straighten their backs to cause a cascading topple of the boulders of possibilities and assurances so many looked to them to fulfill—removing their superwoman capes for preferred attire?

My role as a leader was the heaviest boulder that had me gasping for air as my body volleyed between trying to stay afloat and sinking into an abyss of mis-directed leadership intentions. My reality, even on my worst day, was that any shortcoming in my role as a wife or mother was met with disappointment, but an enduring love in which my children and husband saw me trying to do my best. What I realized about leadership for most of us is that the boulder we don't realize we hold is the intention for our leadership to be a cataclysmic change agent to transform a school or organization. While I didn't want to disappoint my children or husband, it wasn't my intention to be perfect in those roles, but rather, I wanted them to know they were always loved and supported.

As an early leader, I clasped to perfection like the finest of tennis bracelets—full of the brilliance, clarity, and carats to grab the attention of any high-end jewelry customer. My intentions for the people I led was for them to see me as perfect and having solutions to the challenges we faced, and most importantly, to view me as being a credible leader. After years of coaching and supporting hundreds of leaders, I realized the same boulders of shared intentions of mistaking leadership perfection with leadership excellence could handicap even the best of leaders. Having liberated myself from the imposter syndrome, whereas I formed my own boulders and plagued the pathology behind my intentions, I'm committed to helping other leaders do the same and inherit their leadership birthright.

The idea of a person having the right or privilege to a particular item at birth has been around since the beginning of time. The role of an inheritance is often relegated to an actual material possession. In Ghana, West Africa, a birthright perspective is reflected in the principle of Sankofa, centered on the fact that in order for you to know where you are going, you have to know where you are from. The role of cultural and ancestral roots is paramount to guiding one's life, and privileges are passed down from generations as staples to their upbringing, based on gender and birth position.

Similarly, based on biblical Scriptures, in ancient Israel, the oldest son receives a double portion of his birthright. Access to property and authority are bestowed upon birth order. Traditions instituted at birth guide the role of power that is acquired over a lifetime. However, as present-day leaders in our personal and professional lives, we often overlook our birthright and don't reflect enough on the inheritance that comes with the role. As a leader, your ability to navigate power and privilege, without abandoning a servant leadership posture, must be rooted in authentic relationships and equity-centered mindsets and practices. Knowing the needs of the people you lead is essential to your success in empowering them to collectively accomplish outcomes.

As a leader, you must realize that the birthright of leadership is powered by liberation for yourself and the people you lead. Invest in yourself and your people. Inspire yourself and your people. Champion yourself and your people. And hold yourself and your people accountable. The people you inherit deserve your commitment to your continued growth and development, deserve your active disruption of your personal biases and the biases of others, and deserve your untethered journey toward liberation. When you look at transformational leaders such as Sojourner Truth, The Dalai Lama, Mother Theresa, Gandhi, Mandela, Ruth Bader Ginsberg, and Oprah, the quintessential thread between them is their awareness of self and their acknowledgement of humanity.

The dichotomous privilege of leading self and others with grace and a human-centered lens will transform churches, schools, organizations, as well as your families. Within many of our family dynamics, there is something to be said about the delectable generational recipes families pass down. The chef, oftentimes the maternal force in the family who smells like love and cooks like heaven, covets the details of the recipe until someone in the family demonstrates that he or she is worthy to take the culinary baton. This someone, the proverbial collateral with the keys to the kitchen, holds the recipe sacred and turn-keys the responsibility to another recipient in the rising generation. And even if the recipe doesn't exactly taste as good as the original food-god, all future chosen chefs learn to slightly modify the ingredients to meet the needs of the current generation's palate. A clear awareness of the responsibility of the role is assumed, and there is a sense of power in knowing that one was *chosen* to continue the culinary gift for their generation. This power comes with the responsibility to avoid freely giving away the recipe without intention, taking haphazard shortcuts from the suggested ingredients and cook time, and abusing the privilege of knowing the cooktop secrets of one's ancestors. Consider the implications of this example on how you show up as the appointed chef in the kitchen as a leader.

Whether you are leading your family, church, school, or organization, strategically examining how you leverage the ingredients of the people around you to empower, develop, and invest in them, and most importantly, see and hear what they need to actualize their potential, informs how you allow those ingredients to simmer, and subsequently serve the pallets of those that need it most.

Just like you, the people you lead want to know that, as a leader, you have secured safety to help them fail forward, enacted coalitions to help buoy them with a tribe of support, acquired resources to light the path as they navigate challenges, and recognized the honor, privilege, and humanity it will require to uproot personal and collective mindsets and practices along the journey toward liberation.

When you lead with liberation, your leadership becomes a supernova, with an explosion that empowers, affirms, and elevates, even during difficult conversations and staunch accountability. Your course of honoring your birthright requires you to operate as if leadership is your ministry of service and not your elected position of power. As a leader, instead of mainly asking yourself whether you completed the individualized education program meeting, finalized the data reports, or ordered the merchandise refills, begin to also ask yourself: In what ways do my family, friends, and colleagues feel empowered, elevated, and affirmed by me? Reflect on how you model personal liberation of self and others. Initiate those conversations with the people close to you to learn more about how they feel you show up as a partner, sibling, friend, or employee/colleague. Then, take it to the next level and begin the exploration of how you show up as a leader with inquiries such as:

- Who have you empowered to support your new initiative, specifically someone who is often overlooked?
- How can you elevate your most marginalized students, customers, or communities as you facilitate a data review?
- Does your decision, policy, program affirm the cultures and identities of the people you lead?
- In what ways are you prioritizing the well-being and needs of your team?
- What leadership actions do you need to take to disrupt the mindsets and decisions of your team that reinforce systemic barriers and bondage ideologies?

Our transformative self-exploration is designed to shine a light on the dark places in which we often try to seek shade and solace. It isn't enough to do self-work solely based on what people told you about yourself. For instance, you might say to yourself, "I know I'm opinionated. I've heard people tell me this a million times." Or you might think to yourself, "I already know I don't set firm boundaries, which results in others taking advantage of me." The dark places that escape the light are the things others don't feel comfortable telling you about yourself. In fact, we naively hide things from our conscious selves in hopes we successfully mislead our secrets to wander to our subconscious. We have told ourselves counterfeit lies we later try to deposit into delinquent bank accounts. However, once you are on a journey toward freedom, bondage can no longer two-step on your dance floor. You begin to sniff out even the most subtle signs of unethical indoctrination within yourself, as well as in the people and systems around you. Where you once operated with propagandized personal convictions and faulty leadership assumptions, you begin to experience a liberated vibration that transcends your five senses.

The ashes of your former ideologies aren't forgotten, but no longer unhinge your purpose. Your awakening has begun, and your angels and ancestors rejoice. Because you've committed to the process of undoing biases, mindsets, and assumptions that don't serve you and others, your purpose, passions, and peace are the subjects of your liberation love letter. Together, let us begin to chisel away the course conglomerate of fallacy sediments that have formed some of the boulders weighing us down and replace them with liberated scaffolds to lift us up and fuel our leadership intentions, drive our purpose as a leader, and subsequently, contribute to our leadership potential and impact.

chapter three

Untethered by the Intersection of Personal and Professional REALationships

Many of us were raised on the mantra: Relationships come and go, that's life. And while there is some truth to this, the saying should add that relationships operate out of obligations to titles, but *REALationships* are rooted in digging deeper to foster self-discovery, authentic connection, reciprocal growth, and personal development. In 2018, the turning point of my leadership was finding the difference between relationships and *REALationships*. However, it all started on the eve of 2018, days before closing the door on 2017, when I wanted to cast aside my superwoman cape of wife and mothering obligations to re-ignite my enigmatic youth and carelessness.

With the winter holiday break in full swing and the new year around the corner, I was engaged in my normal Christmas activities—a bit naughty, a bit nice. It's interesting how deprivation of the quintessential elements for happiness fuels the conversations you begin to have with the angel on your right shoulder and the commitments you make with the devil on your left. And so, I started 2018 determined to find greater balance in work and life by creating better systems to efficiently get things done. I thought my biggest challenge was to consistently implement those systems, but little did I know then that 2018 was about unearthing the root of a lot of my challenges; most importantly, my challenges with each of my titles. I had my biggest awakening with my title as a wife. In January and February, I began by putting the train on the *right* tracks in my marriage and attempted to do the things I knew would strengthen my relationship with my husband. I did my best to quiet my stubborn contempt of daily routines and planned my husband's 40th birthday trip of a lifetime. In March, I gifted him plenty of stamps in his passport as we voyaged to Kenya, his namesake, Dubai, and Zanzibar for his birthday bucket list.

We dined in the most beautiful restaurants, ate exquisite cuisine, enjoyed breathtaking views, and explored new locales with plenty of sightseeing. It was truly the best adventure. I felt confident wearing my title as wife. A key part of us remaining happy involved me suppressing the urge for spontaneous traveling and committing to more structured financial decisions. We returned from our international bliss and got back into our lockstep of the usual March winter routines: cooking comfort food, indoor playdates with the children, and loaded work schedules to close out the school year.

Little did I know that April of 2018 would bring more than rain showers. I could tell when my life was in a drought. I demonstrated a new level of thirst that could only be satisfied from the fountain of liberation. I sometimes wonder if my ancestors' daily inner voice was centered on screaming for freedom, a top of a rollercoaster kind of scream, a bellowing scream one might yell at a lookout point at the Grand Canyon to let the sound reverberate and bounce across the jagged rocks. Or maybe it was a relentless voice that constantly whispered:

"Run! Jus drop everythin and run. Run fast!"

"Freedom is right around the corner. Don't lose hope – You're gonna be free one day soon. I promise."

"Masta Joseph is takin a likin to ya! It will jus be a matter a time before ya outta dis place or carryin his chile...Just run now – or die tryin..."

Oddly enough, the remnant of that voice echoes a similar tone of what myself and so many of my female friends describe as their daily conundrums trying to balance the various roles in our lives to avoid running away from it all. Why is it that as women, we often wait until we hit rock bottom before we want to attempt to climb toward solid ground? We often choose to be emotionally broke before we shift to seek the land of prosperity. Our inner screams resoundingly say:

- "You're not enough. You don't have what it takes to maintain all of your blessings."
- "Life is hard and everyone's unhappy, so why do you think you deserve something different?"
- "You asked to be a wife and mother and now you're complaining. You should be grateful."

- "God doesn't give you anything you can't handle. Something is wrong with *you* when you can't juggle everything and feel fulfilled."
- "Smile, you're starting to look like what you're going through."

With my inner voice beginning its unforgiving chant, I found myself choking on my dry mouth attempts of a new me, aligned to my new year resolutions in the early months of 2018. The incessant April rain showers didn't come close to quenching my thirst. I attempted to call upon the quiet assertiveness and subtle poise of Michelle Obama but kept unleashing the tenacity and obstinacy of Rosa Parks and Maxine Waters. Seeking a work life harmony seemed unviable. As an early school leader, I became frustrated with non-closure. I had a churning discomfort in my attempt to constantly pour myself into daily responsibilities as an assistant principal. A defeated kink in my chain began to form after meeting with teachers to address concerns, planning events for students, attending meetings, and submitting paperwork beckoned by the central office. Nothing ever felt done!

I sought personal development strategies to address time management and scheduling efficiency with a nonprofit organization. While applying the strategies brought more ease, the greatest awareness I experienced through the process was the importance of scheduling the things on my calendar that sparked joy. My 2018 train began to run more smoothly on its track when I looked at my calendar or received a ping from my phone reminder for events such as:

- Find a student who you see trying to improve and give them a hug.
- Call three parents to highlight progress with their scholar.
- Visit a classroom for 15 minutes to focus on glows and turn off walkie talkie to be present and engage with students while in the classroom.
- Take a walk around the school while taking cleansing breaths to center yourself.

I had to seek out moments of joy and fulfillment amidst the sea of endless responsibilities, sudden emergencies, and tough conversations that peppered the day-to-day grind of leadership. Take a moment to pull out your calendar, phone, a post-it, or pen and schedule at least one moment of joy for the remainder of this week.

Summons the "I think I can" engine of your own personal train and commit to investing in yourself simply by scheduling moments of joy.

As I was basking in landing on resolutions that were working in my professional life, I fell short of solutions for harmony in my personal life. It seemed to be that I couldn't get the planets in my solar system to revolve around my soul sun at the same time. On a parallel train track, the train in my personal life I tirelessly attempted to keep on track in April of 2018 was becoming unhinged. By May, my train was coasting and disobeying all crossing stop lights, without a clear destination. The exhilaration of unencumbered freedom replaced the weariness of the submissive track I was on. To put it bluntly, I was open, wide open. Sometimes when we put vibes of curious desire into the universe, we get back tests and trials to check the extent of our curiosity, which was exactly what happened the evening of May 19th.

Out of curiosity, I went to attend the funeral of an old acquaintance's mother. As fate would have it, I remained friends with people within our friend circles over the years. However, I hadn't physically seen or spoken with Mr. Kumasi in almost 15 years. I had a brief crush on him when in college, but nothing materialized because of my determination to not date and possibly marry an African man. I feared I would be held to traditional African wife roles and have to maintain a posture of submission to thwart being disowned by our families.

Little did I know, my attempts to avoid being submissive came knocking in my current marriage. My fears followed me because I didn't face and dismantle them. Nothing could have prepared me to walk into the funeral that evening. With an air of openness came a certain aroma of confidence. I strutted across the cobble-stoned parking lot, enamored by the sound from the click of my heels and the reflection of my profile in the car windows lined on the lot. As soon as I walked in, and Mr. Kumasi's stature met my gaze for the first time in nearly 15 years, I was taken aback. I had an instant, yet deep emotional connection as I watched him at the head table clothed in black and red attire, the customary Ghanaian funeral garb.

The funeral hall was filled with a mixture of somber cries and faith-based jubilation, and when it became time for the guests to greet the members of the head table, I began to panic and suddenly felt shy. I am far from shy. When it was my turn to greet Mr. Kumasi, I was somehow at a loss for words. My head was screaming praises to the universe for the reunion, and slowly condolences fell from lips like rain drops for his loss. The shock in his eyes signaled that he too was at a loss for words. Soon after, he motioned for me to meet him outside as if a symbiotic understanding were underway. We didn't say much to one another when we stepped outside, but our eyes remained intently glued. We didn't have to say anything. We knew what unsaid wishes were being met and uncommunicated emotions were being shared. Not long after reuniting with Mr. Kumasi, I learned what my ancestor Maya Angelou wrote so eloquently: "Love costs all that we are..." We often think the word "cost" has a negative connotation, but what if the costs my ancestors paid for their liberation weren't intended to be seen as undesirable? What if the ultimate cost by my savior Jesus Christ was in part, intended for us to rethink how we view sacrificial costs?

My 2018 train expedition toward reconnecting with an old acquaintance forced a new journey of self-discovery that led to developing emotional independence, and subsequently influenced my emotional intelligence as a leader. Mr. Kumasi helped to teach me the lesson of the importance of nurturing REALationships, starting with the realest most essential REALationship I will ever have, my REALationship with *myself*. The better you understand and give grace to yourself, the more you are able to cultivate the emotional intelligence required in understanding and giving grace to others, especially the people you lead.

As a strong Black woman who worked hard to overcome growing up in a low-income home with immigrant parents, went on to excel in college, achieved a master's degree and various certifications, and ultimately accomplished my goal of making six figures by the age of 30, I assumed I had emotional independence and the art of understanding people in the bag. The beauty about life is that experiences are often mirrors, revealing to all that gaze upon it hidden struggles, fears, desires, and emotions. In fact, my reflection in the mirror revealed that while I was independent and driven when it came to professional ambition, I was emotionally tethered to the archetypes that created a sense of internal bondage.

As a young adult, I believed doing things the right way would afford me the promises and dreams my ancestors hoped freedom would entail. However, there I was, free and tethered. Free, but scared to grow and explore who I was beyond an educator and leader. Tethered to what being a career woman afforded me. Free, but fearful of what it meant to prioritize my personal happiness.

Tethered to the title of wife and mother because of the joy and accomplishment I felt in raising such phenomenal children and marrying such an amazing man. Free, but consumed by the dogma of upholding the air of religiosity. Tethered to the title of being a pastor's child and Christian. I was free, but not liberated. And so, there I was, running toward Mr. Kumasi for my healing, yet tethered to doing what was familiar, looking outward, instead of looking inward.

I'm grateful for my tribe of friends, eternal sisterhood, that helped to center me at that time and disrupt what I thought was going to bring me clarity. My tribe of friends re-magnetized my compass and sparked an introspective journey to untethering myself from super-imposed expectations, religious fallacies, and charmed fairytales I chased in my titles.

Graduate from high school with good grades. Check. Go to a well-esteemed college and graduate with a career lined up. Check. Go to church every Sunday no matter what. Check. Get married. Check. Buy a house. Check. Start a family. Check. Progress in your career. Check. Oh, if you want checks, I have plenty of them. However, I couldn't checkbox my way through life on a journey toward liberation, no more than anyone can checkbox their way through leading a family, church, school, or an organization to wholeness and wellness. Whole child and whole adult success require commitment to healing your way toward liberation.

Seeking my liberation caused me to take a closer look at the process of healing. At an early age, children are taught to sound the alarm when they get a boo-boo. Parents and caring adults want to quickly ease their pain and immediately heal the wound. It's covered with a band-aid, and children are told to ignore the source of their pain. From that, we learned to seek solace outward for our pain. We believe the answers lie in something or someone else and form dependencies and addictions to things like food, shopping, money, careers, and love. We become tethered. Similarly, how we show up in our personal lives transcends to how we show up in our professional lives. Tethered people, tether people! Consequently, we become leaders ascribing to pushing deadlines, deliverables, and countless directives to meet goals to prove our effective leadership. However, the true success of leaders is measured by the REALationships that are authentically developed with the people they lead.

A tell-tale sign of whether a leader cultivated *REALationship* is seeing the work they led continued once they were gone; evidence the leader-built capacity and empowered their people to take the baton in their absence.

Take a moment to ask yourself, do I build and nurture REALationships with the people I lead and support? Do the people around me feel empowered to hold a high standard that moves the work forward, even in my absence?

Liberated leaders seek and source *REALationship* to cultivate harmony, healing, and wholeness.

Consider your family or friends and determine if you serve as a source of harmony amidst the storms life throws their way. Are you a safe space for them to land, a listening ear for them to confide in, or a loving accountability partner to help ensure they strive to be the best version of themselves? Take into account how you show up in your professional life. Do your words and actions foster healing and forgiveness and empower others to pursue wholeness and wellness? *REALationship* in the workplace promotes higher work outcomes, sustainability, and commitment to excellence. As a leader, if you find the dynamics in your home, family, friendships, and workplace aren't progressing, it's a signal your *REALationship* with yourself and others around you are the barriers to thriving. To address this, lean into your personal leadership growth areas by:

- Exploring the barriers and biases you may have and challenging yourself to be more transparent with yourself and others. The work begins with you.
- Examining the patterns of the *REALationship* you've created with others. Take a closer look at the healthy boundaries you set, or the lack thereof, to ascertain your sustainability. Similarly, evaluating how you hold others accountable while still nurturing healthy *REALationship* with them will reveal the gap in how you show up as a leader who leads with love and lessons. Accountability is an opportunity to reinforce a lesson of growth for yourself and the people you lead.

REALationship require *real* effort,
real vulnerability, and *real* authenticity.

---

chapter four

Untethered by Committing to My Personal Leadership

They say a journey of one mile begins with one step. This could not have been more true of a statement than with my journey toward liberation. Learning to self-indict on the grounds of allowing myself to first conjure up the thoughts of what my growth as a woman meant for myself and others, and then additional indictments on giving myself permission to say my thoughts aloud, led to me to a continuous cycle from trials and tribulations to a closer relationship with God, self-reflection and self-work, followed by true joy and fulfillment, and then back to a repetition of unrelenting trials and tribulations. It was not until I normalized therapy as self-care, even when things were going well, that I learned to find joy and liberation at all phases of life's cycles.

Embracing therapy, even while things were going well, is one of my greatest life lessons.

When my train completely cascaded off the tracks in 2018, I knew it was time to commit to some real self-work. However, as running from myself played out, I anchored my need for therapy in career combustion. I was at a professional crossroad in my role as an assistant principal and felt, while the role was challenging, I wasn't being challenged in areas connected to my purpose. While I knew I was impacting lives in a great way each day, I had a recurring void of wanting a deeper fulfillment aligned to my purpose to serve others. I wanted more. And so, it came to be that I was treading water in the beginning stages of liberation, exploring my purpose, and swimming into the crashing waves of embracing a new narrative of the woman God has called me to be.

Like so many others, when the book *Purpose Driven Life* was released in 2002, I knew what I was reading was colliding with my beliefs. Rick Warren's words were like a testimony of wisdom in a perfectly packaged gift I interpreted as: "Just do this and your life will be all that you want it to be." I became obsessed with the idea of doing things in what I believed to be the *right* way. I've always been a woman of faith. I grew up in the church, and my father graduated from seminary school when I was in high school. When he began to pastor his own church, I believed because I was in church several days a week that the blood of Jesus would fully cover me no matter what. However, when I began to develop my own spiritual *REALationship* with God and started to experience life's personal challenges, I realized my faith walk was a solo experience, and my support network throughout my life was intended to be a buoy, not a preverbal life jacket. You have the power to make decisions that can impact or distract you from your purpose in the same manner you have the power to pick up yourself when you fall.

I am eternally grateful for the various buoys throughout my life. My extended family is loving and a true taste of Africa with everyone they come in contact with. My group of girlfriends are true warriors that have taught me so much and allow me to lean on them to celebrate life's mountaintops and collapse into their arms during life's valleys. My favorite buoys of all time are my children. They are the truest and deepest demonstrations of love that I have ever seen. I know God handpicked them for me, specially and uniquely made with the best parts of me and my husband.

And my husband has indeed been my buoy at times. His uncanny ability to memorize the most, what seems to be miniscule facts, has managed to save us money, time, and peace of mind countless times. I often tell him he is like a walking almanac, constantly internalizing facts and information. He is ready to drop knowledge gems at the drop of a dime. This has been the best conversation starters throughout our marriage. Because I am a naturally curious person, our match was quite befitting. When I want to know something about the weather, my husband, Kenya, addresses my curiosity in great detail, clothing my endless inquiries with accessories, colored fabric, and a great heel to match. When I want to know what caused a particular historical event, Kenya furnishes my vacant wonders with the most elegant of wallpaper, sconces, and window dressings. It was as if those facts were encased in the chasm of his mind, waiting for the slightest opportunity to provide necessary accouterments to any given situation. It didn't matter if the topic was origins of various religions, astrology, criminology, anthropology, historical dynasties, or his ultimate favorite, African American History. When someone has a question, Kenya had the answer.

Conversely, the facts that he did not become fully attuned to were my internal struggles with wanting to be seen and heard. I craved unwarranted hugs and empathetic gazes to fill my emotional cup after a hard day. However, those facts floated away like the feather of a swan riding the wind's syncopated beat as if never to land again. And because at that time, I had not yet fully begun my self-work to reveal what it was that my authentic self needed, I hung onto his facts and hour-long conversations about the stars. I clung to his knowledge like a security blanket, hoping to forever carry the comfort his information provided. However, like all security blankets, they become tattered over time after accompanying their owner to and fro like a "blankey," losing the sense of stability it once provided to a toddler. In fact, it is when toddlers begin to trust their own decision-making more, be it as simple as walking to their parent's room for consolation after a bad dream, that they begin to realize the false safety their "blankey" once provided.

Unbeknownst to me, leaning into therapy at that point in my life helped me to realize I was constructing false safety nets around me because I didn't trust my authentic inner voice. I knew when that voice was screaming, "Freedom is coming!" However, what I didn't know was that when that voice had a calm, hushed intonation in moments of indecisiveness, moments of disappointment, or even moments of fear, I dismissed it. I paid the ultimate price for quieting my inner voice throughout my marriage, which was losing myself. My disappointment that my marriage journey didn't match the movie trailers of my favorite cinemas from the 80s and 90s began forming into a knot of resentment deep in my throat. I wanted reparations from my husband for not experiencing the dynamic I saw emblazoned on the television screen in romantic comedies.

I wanted an endowment of eternal sweet nothings whispered in my ear daily by my husband as a form of consolation for the constant hard work I put into trying to make my marriage, and eventually family, more adventurous and more loving. I wanted acknowledgement from my husband that communicated he saw me and understood how hard it was for me to try to juggle everything as a career woman and mother. However, God doesn't always give you what you want, He gives you what you need, and I needed therapy.

Each of my therapists helped me to me begin removing the tethers of:

- Self-Pity
- Mom guilt
- Resentment
- Body shaming
- Withholding
- Inadequacy
- Relational sabotage
- Hopelessness
- Societal pressures
- Overly ambitious fitness expectations
- Unhealthy work environments
- Negative energy from others
- Plain ol' adulting

Unraveling those tethers has taken years and it continues to be a conscious effort to choose to walk in my purpose, my peace, and my passions each day. I am no longer running from my truth. I am no longer ascribing to the archetype of what others perceive as being a successful woman, wife, mother, or career woman. I am no longer making excuses about why a particular barrier is keeping me from actualizing a goal. I am honoring the experiences and lessons from my past that made me the person that I am today. I am championing the person that I am today and celebrating the woman that I am evolving into.

What are you tethered to? How might you be in your own way by holding fast to one of the tethers above? What sitcom, movie, or social media imagery are you clinging to instead of holding fast to the purpose God has planted within you? Only you can choose to speak your truth and disrupt the tethers you allow to hold you back. Begin soul searching and start conversations with yourself. If you aren't ready to verbalize your truths aloud, journal or jot them on paper.

Name your dark places. Feel your most authentic emotions. You have to go there to transition from there...but you don't have to stay there! Reflect on what you have overcome and learned along your journey and then stamp what you know you are capable of and what living to your fullest potential will look and feel like. Claim your worth and gas up your mental tank because you have an expedition to launch.

Liberation begins with your mindset before your movement. If you haven't been to therapy, I urge you to prioritize this and lean into your odyssey toward your emancipation from tethers. If therapy is something you know you cannot commit to at this time, whether for financial, insurance, or personal reasons, I implore you to seek out a trusted family member, friend, or spiritual leader to begin to tell your story of what makes you who you are. Everyone has a story, and your journey requires you to reflect on the integral moments of your story...the good, the bad, and the ugly, that has shaped how you view the world, others, and most importantly, yourself. Your journey is uniquely yours, and your liberation begins with unpacking it. This unpacking does not have to involve others, you owe it to yourself, to get to know yourself on a deeper level.

Before you can effectively lead others, you have to prioritize your own personal leadership. Taking charge of your life instead of allowing life to happen to you puts you in the driver's seat and equips you to choose to fail forward when challenges arise. The power to choose lies with you.

- Choose gratitude.
- Choose forgiveness.
- Choose work/life harmony.
- Choose optimism.

- Choose kindness.
- Choose being intentional.
- Choose finding joy and fulfillment in the storm.
- Choose therapy.
- Choose healing.
- Choose to do your self- work.
- Choose liberation.

chapter five

Untethered by Assessing How I Show Up for Myself and Others

Our innovation often comes from necessity. Most of us walk through life merely trying to survive and abandon the expectation that life is meant for us to create conditions to help us thrive. We try to keep on our rose-colored glasses for as long as possible. Yet, the inescapable harsh realities of life often blur those glasses well earlier than we are ready, and our fight for constant survival begins. When did you shift into survival mode? When did you stop trusting in the people and things around you and began to cling to an emerging self-reliance or a deeper faith rooted in your relationship with God, your ancestors, and/or the universe?

Interestingly enough, life can sometimes make you wonder if you can trust *yourself*. Think about the most recent instance in which you *knew better* but chose not to *do better*. Your moment might have been years ago, but for some of us that are truly a work in progress, our moment could have been minutes ago. Those instances may have ranged from extreme to minuscule, but all the same, they were when we weren't our best selves.

During our moment, we challenged our inner voice and the world around us in a defiant manner because we thought the risk far outweighed the reward. Since we are tearing off proverbial band-aids together, I willingly accept my vulnerable moment and recall one of the earlier times in my life when I started to put on the cloak of survival as life started to clip the petals from my rose-colored glasses. Little did I know, my rose petals and their roots would forge their way through cemented ambitions and thoughts of discontentment for decades.

I learned early that growing up poor created a cavity of constant want and yearning inside and impacted the way I interpreted the world. I ran from every circumstance in my life that could possibly return me back to a state of lack. I grew up in Brockport, New York in an apartment complex called Viking Way. Upon entering the complex, you would see the dirt-brown multi-story buildings and children peppered around the playground in the midst of a double-dutch challenge, a game of hide and go seek, or sandbox wars.

Despite being poor, I had a fun childhood. Like many 80s babies, our existence was centered on playing outside from sunup until sundown. Ashia, my older sister who served as my protector and second mother, and I left the apartment before 9:00 in the morning, and somehow the bowl of cereal mixed with milk and water, in hopes to stretch the milk until mom could afford to go grocery shopping again, sustained us long enough to return home when it started to get dark.

The meager accommodations of Viking Way, which became home for many immigrants and college students, were what many called low-income housing. Yet, to us, they were a child's dream. The area was surrounded by canopied woods and bountiful dirt hills. The slopes served as our summer water slides in the absence of having enough money to venture to the water park during summer break. The grounds of Viking Way became our ultimate theme park adventure. We lacked monetary richness, yet, we had priceless childhood amusement. On any given day, I relentlessly begged someone to borrow a boombox, the source of titillated joy for most early 80s babies and spent hours making up dances with my best friend LaShannah, who til this day has spun friendship and sisterhood into a lyrical web of the perfect ride or die anthem for our close bond. We gyrated to the percussion of Lisa Lisa Cult Jam's "Wonder If I Take You Home" and Paula Abdul's "Straight Up" until beads of sweat became drenched odors of outdoor pursuits. When we grew tired of dancing holes in our shoes along the sidewalk, we walked to a neighboring college campus where my mother was doing a different type of dance. She taught African dance at Suny Brockport College in Upstate New York. The campus was a second home for us.

We felt celebrity status affiliation to be able to say we knew thee Edna Mensah, and proudly let Mommy roll off of our tongues like treasured dice toppled onto a Russian roulette table. In fact, various Ghanaian professors like Dr. Ocansey and Dr. Okoye welcomed us whenever we frequented the campus. The African community at the college and surrounding area was our safe haven. Our chocolate brown skin was affirmed, we reveled in our parents *thique* accents, and the unique aromas of our foods filled the apartment hallways across Brockport.

Now, to avoid your possible wonderings about my experiences growing up poor while my mother worked at a college, you have to understand the context of how it came to be that my Kente-clothed Ghanaian mother, with a billowing, yet majestic accent that poured over her lips like sap from an African palm tree, was a college dance instructor during the 70s. Before I begin to share *her* story, I have to begin with the caveat that my mother is truly my favorite person in the *entire* world. I am a momma's girl through and through. My mother, Edna Mensah, is the gift my ancestors wrapped perfectly for my siblings and me, knowing her untamed humor and relentless optimism would fill our lives like potpourri, designed to hide what truly laid beneath her struggle to actualize the American Dream. We didn't feel poor. Our mother loved us so deeply that the joy she brought was as palatable as the large pot of Ghanaian peanut butter soup she sat atop the stove in our small Viking Way kitchen for days as our only source of nourishment when we especially wanted on our pallets was a full-course American meal like meatloaf and mashed potatoes. To this day, whenever I make meatloaf, I chuckle as I remember being a child and seeing such a basic, cost-effective American meal. It was the dinner centerpiece on every 1980s sitcom like *Punky Brewster, Full House, and Gimme a Break,* episode after episode. I watched those television shows entranced by what I thought it meant to live an American life as I glanced at our stovetop filled with another pot of mom's soup.

Oddly enough, I now delight in the experience while cooking and eating authentic Ghanaian food, having liberated myself from the societal ideals of what being American actually means. Truth be told, Edna Mensah didn't make it easy for us to subdue our African roots. She appeared at our school for a holiday chorus concert in full traditional African attire from head to toe and during my countless sleepovers, she brought my friends and me our refreshments perfectly balanced on a tray on top of her head as she danced to herself beatboxing African drums, leaving my friends in utter shock at the seemingly circus-infused mother they saw before them.

I appreciated my Spencerport Elementary School girl squad for staying composed enough during my sleepovers to not make me feel ashamed of my mother, but also committed enough to resounding laughter to affirm my mother's efforts to entertain us. My bestie Chermaine (Choo-Choo) with her almond-colored Latina skin leaned back in her neon tie-dyed shirt, laughing under her breath, while my other bestie Amy's (Tweety's) freckled face lit up as she jumped up to dance alongside my mother, and my now eternal angel bestie, Melissa (Bam-

B), and I collapsed onto the nearby furniture, be it my twin bed or our velvet snake-shaped couch, with resounding hysterical giggles. At our early age, we knew my mother was a force.

My mother was born in Ghana, West Africa, in a small town outside of Accra called Labadi, which was named by the European poachers that arrived on the shores of Ghana in the 15th Century. Frustrated with the strong-will and fortitude of the people in the surrounding Accra area, they named them "La bad" people, meaning the bad people. Referring to Ghanaian locals in that manner signaled newer settlers to proceed with caution. It's galling that settlers were apprehensive about Ghanaians when *they* were the ones unjustly invading the land with their false claims of manifest destiny. Unfortunately, the misnomer of 'La Bad' remained well after the treasonous invaders left the shore. It is my hope that one day, similar to how some townspeople across the U.S. are removing statues and renaming buildings and schools previously named after historic figures that committed racist acts against humanity, Labadi will also be renamed to honor the rich culture and family-oriented traditions of its people.

Portuguese settlers coined the area the Gold Coast because of its bountiful gold mines. Overlooking the wealth of the people, culture, and traditions of Ghana, they ravaged the mines, depleting much of the area's capital and raping the prosperity and affluence in the region, which is still felt today. However, gold wasn't the most valuable resource stolen from the shores of Ghana. The tears and cries of my ancestors still beat upon the waves across the Atlantic Ocean from Labadi Beach. The ancestral ties from the region created a tapestry of circumstance-defying fervor within my mother at a very young age. One of 10 children, my mother experienced the loss of her parents at a young age and poverty to the extent to make my childhood home in Viking Way look like a sprawling Beverly Hills mansion in comparison.

Raised by her older siblings, my mother was often disciplined for not spending enough time focused on her schoolwork and too much time dancing in the streets and anywhere she could conjure up a crowd willing to spare loose change. To this day, at nearly 80 years of age, my mother only needs to hear the downbeat of any song, and by the third beat she is up with sweeping strides and articulated arm gestures, capturing any audience.

I don't believe in luck. God orchestrates all things according to our purpose and it's our job to be prepared and open to walking in it. This is the essence of liberation. My mother often tells us the story of how she *danced* into her purpose from being selected in a dance audition at a local university in Ghana in the 60s. She was first turned away because she didn't own dance shoes, but her unparalleled talent convinced the international judges that the melodic antelope leaps and syncopated tribal stomps of the orphaned dancer before them was exactly what the dance program of Suny Brockport College in upstate New York needed.

With few belongings, my mother boarded the plane for the United States, forever changing the trajectory of our family and her legacy. Now, as a mother myself, I realize the love and joy she raised us with was seasoned with a deeper knowing of the sacrifices of her past, which serves as constant reminders of what was and the hope for unprecedented favor and potential for what could be.

As a child, my sister and I clamored backstage behind the curtain at a Suny Brockport Dance Performance watching my mother and her dance troupe color what originally was an auditorium filled with the sounds of classical ballet and Eurocentric movements to the gyrating beats of African drums and rhythmic body movements, forever changing how dance was defined not only on campus, but worldwide. My mother danced for acclaimed artists such as Fela Kuti and led dance ensembles alongside the renowned Garth Fagen, known for his choreography on the Broadway musical, *The Lion King*. My mother and her dance troupe were supported by the African community of Brockport from the likes of the late Dr. Okoye to Clyde Morgan. They played an integral role in bringing her dream to become a professional dancer to fruition.

My mother held fast to her dreams that were forged dancing barefoot in the streets of Ghana as she traveled the world from Italy to Mexico, even performing for the then-president, Richard Nixon. Yet, as many performers often said, their popularity did not always equate to financial prosperity. Viking Way remained our reality during my mother's tenure as a dance instructor at Suny Brockport College. While she was the most gifted dance mom in town, we were among the lower class of constituents. We didn't have much, but the African community in Brockport was tight knit and our weekends were often filled with dance parties to African Highlife music until the sun rose. Mom continued to visit Ghana every year after coming to the U.S. until the dance program began to evolve and she looked for other, more stable, career opportunities.

Soon after, my brother and sister, Eric and Trudy, and our father, Jordan, immigrated to the United States, we moved to Spencerport, a suburban area approximately 30 minutes from Brockport. During that transition, my awareness of being of the lower economic class began to show up in my thoughts and fears. Moving away from the Brockport African Dance Community that sustained us immediately catapulted me into a pool of internal conflict and tension. I felt ill-equipped to exist in the Spencerport School District. Chermaine, Melissa, and Amy, lest not forget one of my brightest constellations, LaShannah, were my saving grace during my years in Spencerport. My cloak of survival adorned me on most days existing around peers whose lives mirrored what I saw on sitcoms so many nights in Brockport as I reluctantly swallowed mom's soup for the week. At every crack in my life's concrete, my rose petals challenged the sun and pushed through on my journey toward liberation. I harbored haunting questions. Do I belong here? Most importantly, do I deserve to be here?

Although I acquired beautiful friendships and countless memories during my time in Spencerport, I gained a distinct awareness of my Blackness and how it was perceived by others. Teachers and staff made numerous comments to me that I couldn't fully grapple with at the time—the thorns on my roses. In elementary school, Mrs. R pulled me aside when I got in trouble at recess.

"Leslie, you are starting to act more and more like them," as she pointed her pale, vein-strewn fingers to several African American students. "I thought you were different, but if you're going to act like that kind, I won't choose you to read to the kindergarten classes anymore."

I was confused as she scolded me. Up until that moment, Mrs. R was one of my favorite teachers. She often called on me when I raised my hand in class and let me help grade my peers' assignments. However, in that moment, I realized the privileged treatment I experienced from Mrs. R was because she wanted me to be different from the stereotypes she constructed about the other students that looked like me. In addition, the comments from some of the parents of the white students with whom I befriended also accessorized my self-awareness. "That's your mother, the one with the towel on her head?" one said.

I was too embarrassed to explain that it was African cloth adorned as a headwrap like the crown of Queen Nefertiti. Instead, I drew my embarrassment inward and worked to overcompensate to prove I wasn't one of them. I didn't want them to fear picking up the black or brown crayon in the box, determined not to tarnish the pale palette of their illustrated masterpiece embedded within their child. I wanted to convince those parents that my Blackness wasn't contagious and the African braids I embellished to match my attire weren't a bad influence. I too had hopes, fears, good grades, and age-appropriate mischief...just like their child. In Malcolm X's words in his speech "Who Taught You to Hate Yourself?" painstakingly seduced my inner child with his bombastic tone:

> "Who taught you to hate the texture of your hair? Who taught you to hate the color of your skin? To such extent you bleach, to get like the white man. Who taught you to hate the shape of your nose and shape of your lips? Who taught you to hate yourself from the top of your head to the soles of your feet?"

If only I could tell Mrs. R that the words she spoke over me, intentional or not, branded me like cattle for decades to come. As a sixth grader, I was hurled into a world of self-doubt, far from the realizations of the power of my ancestors. However, through her unchecked biases, she helped me to birth an under-dog persona within me, and that fostered my commitment to always doing my best to perform at a high level in everything I pursued. Mrs. R's fear of my skin embedded a fear of failure within me that I still work to tame today. I'm grateful for the families of people like Amber Nuzny, Becky Hill, and Chermaine Ramos. They helped to make me feel welcome in their homes during my elementary school days. I vividly remember sitting comfortably at the dinner table with their families. I'm eternally grateful they weren't afraid to choose the black and brown crayons in those early years.

We often don't realize the gravity of how a particular bias we have can make others feel. The same is true of how we show up as leaders. Our biases help to shape the remnants of intent and impact over the people we lead. Take a moment and consider when you may have acted out of assumption, stereotype, or bias with someone that may be harboring resentment or hurt feelings as a result of an interaction with you. Choose restoration in this moment, and if you are ready, give them a call, schedule time to meet in person, or at least journal a message to apologize for not offering grace, understanding, or tolerance when they needed it. Liberate them from the branding you may have placed on them and commit to your continued growth and awareness in a manner that inspires others to do likewise. Once we experience true liberation, it is our duty to set others free.

As an early leader, I found myself subconsciously demonstrating favoritism toward staff members with whom I perceived shared similar work ethic and interests as me. I invested more time with those staff members and exhibited interest in encouraging them to become more innovative and creative in the classroom. It wasn't until I completed a battery of leadership inventories during a leadership development session that I learned about the leadership attributes and biases I embodied. Some of the attributes I fully embraced and felt affirmed who I believed I was at my core. Traits such as taking initiative, innovative, and decisive consistently surfaced in multiple inventories.

However, my self-perception was wounded when I discovered my leadership blind spots: struggled to hold others accountable, avoided confrontation, prioritized pleasing others, and established inconsistent boundaries. I was tethered to showing up as the leader others wanted and didn't effectively balance it with the leader they needed. I wrestled with the implications of what was revealed in the inventories about the parts of me I didn't acknowledge. Soon after, I sought out additional feedback from diverse groups of people with whom I had led in the past and was leading at the time, and chose to do three things with the data I discovered about my leadership strengths and growth areas:

1. Prioritize time for my continued professional development to build my capacity as a leader through training, classes, and research.
2. Lean into doing the self-work that is required to show up as an equity-centered leader, beginning with seeking out mentors to help me address my blind spots.
3. Strategically leverage others around me that had strengths in areas where I was weak, fully embracing the dynamic of building a diverse team with a range of leadership styles and perspectives.

Most importantly, I choose healing. I made the intentional decision to forgive Mrs. R along with the numerous other educators that, unbeknownst to them, helped to give my rose the fortitude it needed to demolish the concrete around me. The seeds of self-doubt and imposter syndrome they planted in me at an early age were a part of my journey, but not the final chapter of my book. My revelations support my continued healing and help to shape the level of resilience that transformative leadership requires.

chapter six

Untethered by the Gift and Curse of Leading for Liberation

"Birds flyin' high, you know how I feel
Sun in the sky, you know how I feel
Breeze drifftin' on by, you know how I feel

It's a new dawn
It's a new day
It's a new life for me, yeah
And I am feeling good!"

Some of us have morning traditions we employ to start our day. The more I developed as a leader, the more I refined my morning routine to choose to begin the day with intention. I began with a morning prayer of gratitude for being gifted with a new day of opportunities complimented with some good ole Nina Simone melodies with songs like "Feeling Good." As a way to reimagine what a sense of optimism was for the day, I had to center on what I hoped the day would be and how I wanted to show up as a leader, without dwelling on the realities of the hardships from the previous day. I had to choose to approach each day with a renewed sense of opportunity, decide to modify my convictions for a new day based on failing forward, and opt to embrace both the gifts and curses that come with leadership.

There is no better personal development than the process of leading others, all while addressing areas of growth in them that reflect back to the darkest places within you. As a leader, you may find yourself helping others actualize things you struggle to replicate in your own life. You may use your platform to help others navigate insurmountable obstacles and elevate others to honor their excellence. Yet, as leaders, we often fail to celebrate our own small wins and prioritize our own sustainability. As life always plays out, you learn what you live. And through one lived experience in particular, I realized that one of the most profound gifts of leading others is self-leadership.

During my tenure as a master educator, I evaluated English language arts and social studies teachers in grades kindergarten through twelfth. While it was my role to assess their effectiveness in facilitating learning experiences for their students, I often found myself being put under a microscope and challenged. During the initial years of this evaluation program, I was met with inquiries about my age, the college where I graduated, and even if English was my first language. Challenging the credibility of leadership is the oldest trick in the book, but it's funny how even the most common personal attacks can trigger childhood wounds, the ones we failed to lick that festered and rotted their way into our adulthood. Take a moment and think about a past professional experience with a colleague, employee, or peer that proved to challenge your support, disrupt what you believed to be true about your effectiveness as a leader, and in essence, exposed your personal wounds. What exactly was it about what was said or done that demagnetized your leadership compass from your personal North Star?

Managing the gifts and curses that come with leadership depend on how well we navigate our rotating pivot as the needle of our own compass. Leadership is people business. Embrace being a leader for the people. To be our best leader self, we must respect those we lead, believe in their potential, empower them to actualize it, and most importantly, explore their values and convictions. People need to know that what matters most to them is something that we value as well.

As a leader, when you lean into leading with excellence, you are bound to feel the pull of magnets around you. After all, compasses are pulled by magnetic fields and are affected by other electrical sources. Because opposites attract, you may find yourself in a push and pull dynamic with leading others that have an opposing vision, a contrary work ethic, or possibly a deficit mindset, disrupting the morale and well-being within your family, school, or organization. To dig deeper into the motivations behind an individual or groups of individuals you are leading, it's essential you first center yourself on your leadership compass. Explore what motivates, triggers, and challenges you, and the unyielding reason behind it all. Before you can serve others, begin weaving together the layers of your own fabric.

Being an effective leader involves a constant posture of service amidst opposing forces, which could be viewed as a curse of leadership. However, we must shift our mindset to begin each new day as a human-centered leader choosing to lead with intention. Like Nina Simone, a leader examines the beauty of each new day with the birds flying, the sun shining, the breeze blowing...and the people pulling right, tugging left, pushing south, and lifting north, and still chooses to remain centered on the compass.

Feeling good is measured by how you lead...in spite of. Embrace how you will show up as your best leader self, in the face of having to navigate ambiguity in uncertain times, personal hardships, limited resources, financial strain, and mental health challenges abounding during the year. You are a leader who gets back up, even after being knocked down by various forces. Your only competition is the best version of your leadership self. Leading 4Liberation requires a level of humility in knowing you are serving and learning from others, while simultaneously leading them. Celebrate your strength, resilience, and fortitude that has brought you thus far. Leadership is hard and often lonely. However, you have the power to choose to leverage the people you lead to promote or deter your vision. People know when you view them as an investment or barrier to your intended goal. Regardless of where they fall on that line of demarcation, lead....in spite of.

I once had a supervisor who, within the first minutes of meeting her for the first time, repeatedly stated, "I make people better. Trust me. If you are willing to learn from me, you will get better."

And while I don't believe she had any ill-intentions, I realized she hadn't fully begun her journey toward liberation. She lacked an understanding of being both a resource and a vessel for me, as well as our team, and as a result, the team disbanded soon after she assumed her leadership role.

Leading as a Resource

Leading 4Liberation involves you being a resource and a vessel. When you wake up each day aiming to be both, your perspective of how you live your life and show up as a leader will shift. Being a resource for others translates to building the capacity of the people you lead to being a resource, not only to themselves, but also for other stakeholders in the school or organization. This will magnify your impact as a leader and the outcomes your school or organization aims to achieve. Being resourceful isn't to be misconstrued with mainly having access to resources or sharing a multitude of them. It's essential to be strategic with the resources you secure. In other words, centering yourself on your compass when your North Star is liberation begins with establishing a shared vision of where the promise-land destination is for your school or organization. The people you are leading want to know you are authentically invested in their journey to the extent you want to unearth the experiences that reveal the narrative of where they've been and then, collaboratively discuss data that informs where they aim to go next. You won't know if you are a resource if there hasn't been a shared vision of where your school or organization is going, what the goals and milestones will be to actualize that vision, how success of the goals will be measured, and an in-depth discussion about what key stakeholders of the vision need to help them get there.

As the leader, you then can re-magnetize your compass to serve as a resource to establish the support needed for the voyage. To this end, you cannot coin yourself as being a leader who makes people better when there is an absence of systems and structures in place to create agency for your school or organization to be a part of shared decision-making. No one wants a leader who has a deficit orientation on how he or she empowers others to become better. Once you have the shared vision for the destination and engage diverse stakeholders in a deep dive into the demands and needs to accomplish the vision, you and other members of your leadership team are then able to strategically secure resources in a manner that promotes success. Resources help to liberate the people you lead when they:

- Remove systemic barriers and address biases that can disrupt or delay the shared vision.
- Build capacity of those you lead to demonstrate excellence and work toward mastery in a particular area.
- Differentiate the learning and development available throughout the journey to ensure you are meeting stakeholders where they are and pushing their practice to another level.
- Align to culturally responsive practices to address the context in which the strategies to meet the vision will be applied.
- Elevate the well-being and sustainability of those stakeholders that are working toward the vision.

During my tenure as an assistant principal, I supported my teachers and leadership team in implementing literacy initiatives. One of the chief reasons we made profound gains with Common Core English Assessments during the school years between 2016 and 2019 was due to the number of equity-centered resources available to support the work. The resources weren't just literacy guidebooks, exemplars, lesson plan samples, and classroom anchor charts. The staff members turn-keyed content from our literacy-focused professional development sessions into their smaller professional learning cohorts, observed a peer to provide feedback on the literacy practices we were implementing, normed on scoring practices, and jointly worked to analyze student data to monitor progress. Students and families had agency through student work presentations, feedback surveys, and celebrations like literacy night and parent-led seminars. District leaders were invited in to observe our literacy data adorned through the hallways and evaluate curriculum alignment through feedback rounds. Community partners that leveraged literacy skills in their careers served as guest speakers and school field trips were designed for real world literacy applications.

Our vision for literacy integration was successful because of the additional resources, both human capital and research-based resources. However, keep in mind that the well of resources can also dry up. It is imperative that the same energy put into strategic planning for measures of success to monitor progress, matches that same energy you apply to factoring in sustainability measures. Consider the following questions when you are enacting a shared vision:

- What distributive leadership systems must be in place to have shared accountability of the vision and what does your role as a resourceful leader look like to help make it happen?
- What self-care strategies and healing-centered protocols will be employed in order to support sustainability for others to enact the vision, including yourself?
- What leadership actions do you need to take to ensure your compass is centered on personal liberation and the liberation of others?

Leading as a Vessel

Most leaders gravitate toward being a resource to share information or skills with others, or at least point the people they lead in the direction to access a resource. However, being a vessel is not as easily embraced. For some of us, we connect to our faith and spirituality submit to a level of selflessness to serve as a vessel to allow God to use us for His purpose. I often pray for God to use me for His glory because I know my wellbeing, happiness, and ability to serve others can only happen with and through Him. However, in full transparency, our ego often causes us to choose to take the easier or more assured route than to step onto a vessel-laced tight rope.

Submitting to being used as a vessel for a greater purpose requires humility and faith amidst the unknown. Regardless of your spiritual orientation, being a vessel is beyond religion because it is rooted in relationships. Vessel-centered relationships shift liberated leaders from: "Just trust me" to "I trust where you're trying to go with this idea. What do you need from me to help you get there?" Vessel-centered relationships give recognition to the team, even before the intended outcome hasn't been fully realized. It's a faith walk to empower others to captain the ship at times without reaching for the wheel when the waves get too rough.

Leading for liberation is your chance to be the peace in the midst of the storm, even as the ship bows to and fro. It's the time for the people you lead to know you trust them, are rooting for them, and are positioning the sails to promote their success. Most importantly, it's the time to show them you aren't laser focused only on whether the vision is achieved, but rather, the process, their wellness, and the collective learning along the journey toward the vision. Actualizing the dynamic of being both a resource and vessel will shape the tapestry of the gifts and curses of your leadership journey.

Take a moment to reflect on an initiative or project you are currently leading. How can you reposition the sails of the project to better serve as a resource *and* a vessel? Which stakeholder might you need to meet with to better understand how they need you to angle their sails? Who might you need to call or email to express your gratitude and faith in their role in the initiative or project? This is what having a transformative impact as a leader looks like in action, which is elevating the needs of the people you lead and not your own agenda—living and leading for liberation.

I began this chapter with Nina Simone's lyrics of optimism, and it's only right to close this chapter honoring the liberation that awaits us all with her song, "I Wish I Knew How It Would Feel to Be Free."

"I wish I knew how it would feel to be free
I wish I could break all the chains holdin' me

I wish I could give all I'm longin' to give
I wish I could live like I'm longing to live

I wish I could do all the things I can do
And though I'm way overdue
I'd be startin' anew"

Thank you for your commitment to starting anew! Choosing to live and lead with liberation is a new dawn and a new day.

chapter seven

Untethered by Pandemic Pedagogy

The spread of the COVID-19 virus in the spring of 2020 shook us to our core. The realization of just how vulnerable we are as humans triggered fears many had clothed with delusive contentment and colorless rainbows for so long that truths became myths. The pandemic lockdown provoked the inner giants that took up space in our minds, and many of us hadn't taken the time to slay. Our inner giants stomped about the kitchen, joining us on relentless trips to the fridge to feed our fears of what it meant to live during a pandemic. They joined us on the couch as we cascaded through social media platforms to explore virtual pipe dreams, allowing us to temporarily escape the mounting Covid death tolls illustrated on the nightly news. Fear became a universal language for the rich, poor, and the rest of us in between, in a way that it hadn't before.

By the onset of the summer months, the fog of the drastic transition to virtual learning and the daze of alien stares from other masked constituents began to wear off as we scoured the aisles of the grocery store. Many of us began to lean into the slower pace of our remote work schedules. When summer break began, we no longer had the double-dutch pressure between managing our children while they engaged in virtual instruction along with the work tasks we were responsible for completing with excellence.

Our systems of survival started to get replaced with increased awareness of personal wellbeing and the investment in the welfare of others. The phrases "Give yourself grace" and "Check on your strong friends" went viral on social media. And while many of us started to realize the time came to begin the heavy lifting required to slay our internal giants, the tug of war between life as it had been prior to the pandemic and as it was playing out during the pandemic became a daily battle.

While it's understood that hardship and journeys through the valleys in life are designed to reveal what we are made of, the trauma associated with the pandemic hit many of us close to home and was unforgiving to the most marginalized members of our communities. Leaders tried to pivot and implement trauma-responsive practices to scale across their schools or organizations. Our return to in-person learning and work schedules exacerbated the already overwhelming role of leadership. Early morning meetings and greetings of students, families, and staff were compounded with countless Covid-19 protocol trainings and contact tracing calls.

Our leadership excellence shifted to highlight operational leadership in a manner most leaders were unfamiliar with. The reigning skillset of choice was ground-zero management. Take a moment to celebrate the fact that you survived...all...of...that! However, the integral change agent that shifts just surviving to thriving is reflecting on the lessons learned during survival-mode in order to apply different solutions moving forward. If there is one key lesson we should've have learned from leading during the pandemic, it should be that personal wellbeing and supporting the welfare of others are paramount.

I shifted my understanding of the adage: "You are only as strong as your weakest link" to "You are truly only as strong as your ability to control your inner giants in order to liberate your mindset and the mindsets of others." The power of my mindset was reinforced because of the pandemic. Hope, faith, and the belief that it was time to establish a new normal gave me the license to start anew. As leaders, we often mainly look for the results of our effectiveness in others instead of evaluating our personal mindsets and decisions to analyze the root causes. With self-evaluation comes self-work, so we often project our fears of doing the work to primarily focus on the results around us. Leading for liberation is rooted in developing your personal leadership and your commitment to self-work that improves how you show up as an equity-centered leader. Addressing the following internal personal leadership areas will lead to the external results and outcomes we all long to bring to fruition as leaders:

Embrace Continuous Healing

To effectively implement healing-centered practices in your family, school, or organization, you must champion those practices yourself. You cannot teach someone to value healing, forgiveness, good counsel, and mindfulness when you don't see the value in it. Not only is it beginning each day with intention and centering yourself on your compass, but it also involves practices such as therapy, mindfulness breathing and meditation exercises, the restoration of broken relationships, apologizing and choosing to forgive others that might not gain the courage to apologize to you...the list goes on. Healthy habits such as avoiding settings that trigger your traumas, verbalizing your feelings instead of internalizing them, and prioritizing time for you to reset at various points in the day will allow you to practice and apply self-healing techniques.

Invest In Developing Your Emotional Intelligence

Leaders raised in an environment where self-expression and emotions weren't affirmed and/or emotions weren't valued in a professional setting, often hinder their personal potential and growth due to a lack of emotional intelligence. The people you lead rely on you to serve as a model of self-awareness and relational management. As affirmed by researchers, leaders that show instances of vulnerability and humility with the people they lead, build trust. Clasping to perfection as a leader creates a chasm between you and those you lead, subsequently jeopardizing their ability to view you as an equity-centered and credible leader. Meeting the needs of others is your superpower, and it begins with knowing yourself at a deep level.

Calibrate A Pathology for Liberation

Liberation is a mindset, before you act on it. Your mental pathology is rooted in the patterns of mental behaviors you've established. To disrupt unhealthy patterns, you must replace them with positive habits to promote the person and leader who you aim to be. Creating a vision board isn't enough. You must re-imagine what liberation means to you and how you want to actualize it in your life. New mental habits include things such as positive self-talk superseding your inner childhood trauma voice, mental cleansing overriding mental overload, meditation/stillness disrupting being overworked, and a deeper faith in your potential erasing defeat. Creating a new pathology and pattern won't be easy. Grant yourself grace during the process. Pair your mental shift with actions such as posted notes to illuminate reminders of your new pattern, quotes to reaffirm your new self, recruit family and friends to uplift and encourage you on your new journey, and apply new self-care techniques such as healthier food choices, fitness, and altered scheduling options like getting up earlier to begin your day with something that brings you joy. Making room in your life for a more connected, authentic, and liberated version of yourself embraces the global awakenings charged within us as a result of the pandemic. The work is yours and yours alone. However, you aren't alone in the process of planting seeds of liberation that will come to fruition not only in your life, but in the lives of others around you. Be sure to write today's date in your self-workbook in Chapter 8. Today is the day that you gave yourself more permission to step into your purpose, your peace, and your passions!

chapter eight

Untethered by Living and Leading Liberation (Self- Workbook)

Living with purpose, passion, and peace are your inheritance. Not only is it your right, but you deserve a life to be conscious and committed to unlocking your potential and the potential of others. In this chapter, you will have the opportunity to engage in an inventory questionnaire to help you to get closer to aligning with your North Star toward liberation. As a leader, you are likely familiar with strengths-finders or personality questionnaires. Power is in the process of knowing. We often become intrigued when a realization from a questionnaire or inventory forces us to acknowledge a certain part of ourselves that we haven't yet uncovered.

Because a core part of liberating yourself and others is connected to removing barriers and disrupting deficit pathologies, this reflection workbook will help you take off the self-imposed band-aids referenced in the prologue. The workbook prompts are intended to help you dig deeper into your self-awareness and avoid shrinking your potential by settling for just surviving life. Liberation makes thriving the standard. The workbook is intended to remind you of who you are and to fuel the person and leader you are on the path to becoming. This is your season for radical liberation! Let's begin with reflecting on your essence that informs how you show up in your personal and professional lives.

Begin By Looking Back

In order to know where you are going, healing and clarity begin by embracing the lessons from where you've been. Liberating yourself from your past plays a key role in making peace with your journey of learning through life's experiences. Looking back is about honoring the person you were and expressing gratitude for the valleys, mountain tops, and everything in between that was designed purposely for you. No one else could have lived your life. Your journey is uniquely yours. Let us begin with unpacking the layers of where you've been.

Reflect on at least one instance when you felt a strong sense of pride in yourself for accomplishing something or overcoming a challenge. Jot your experience and a brief description of what attributed to your resolve with navigating this circumstance.

____

____

____

____

____

____

____

____

Center On Your Earlier Memories of Love or Joy

Reflect on one instance of love or joy that gave you a sense of security and fulfillment during your younger years. Who or what was it that helped you feel seen, heard, present, and or appreciated in that experience? Jot notes and capture why the experience was fulfilling.

____

____

____

____

____

____

____

____

Center On a Significant Obstacle from Your Past That You Allow to Influence Your Present

Reflect on an area of your life you are currently struggling to navigate. Push yourself to go deeper to explore the root reasons why you are challenged by this area of your life. Prompt yourself to go back to your early childhood and/or early adulthood to think through similar challenges that connect to this area in your life. Understanding your triggers and the strongholds that make you feel stuck or defeated will empower you to confront mindsets that keep you from liberating those roots.

- What area of your life is out of alignment with a better version of yourself?

- How is this area impacting your personal and professional life?
- What barrier(s) are in your way that keep you from showing up as your authentic self in this area?

Jot reflections to these prompts and push yourself to uproot the deeper challenge stemming from this area.

____

____

____

____

____

____

____

____

Center on the Origin of Your Fears

Your fears can be leveraged to stretch you beyond your self-imposed limitations. However, most of us lean into fears in a manner that is debilitating and contrary to developing the best version of ourselves because we feel safer and more protected when we stay within the parameters of our fears. What are two to three of your most prominent fears causing you to limit your ability to live and lead with liberated mindsets, beliefs, and actions? Push yourself to go deeper and think about past circumstances when you became bound by your fears. Jot reflections to capture how your fears developed and what you believe you were protecting yourself from.

____

____

____

____

____

Come Full Circle

Now that you had the opportunity to center on your resolve, joys, and fears from your past, reflect on how those experiences create internal and/or external barriers in your personal and professional life today. What is one ambition or goal you would like to accomplish in the coming months? What internal and/or external barriers do you need to disrupt to strengthen your resolve as you pursue your ambition/goal?

Look Ahead

What does actualizing your purpose, peace, and passions look like in action? Call out to your future self. Speak life into your future self. Embrace your power to step into your future self. Avoid limiting the reality of your future self to an ultimate destination that will take years to reach. Your future isn't one singular end point, but a continuous expansion of your authentic self you will continue to bring into fruition moments, days, months, and even years from now. Let's begin nurturing your future self now, embracing the full journey of your evolution.

Center On Archetypes and Titles You Need to Abandon

What personal beliefs about your authentic self do you want to embrace? What current beliefs do you wish to abandon in your future? For instance, if you currently hold the belief, you will be miserable if your future self is not married but want your future self to embrace finding joy whether you are single or married, jot notes about shifting your mindset to be self-assured in your future. False archetypes limit the potential of you becoming your authentic self. What are the archetypes you need to desert to actualize the future self that you want to achieve?

Come Full Circle & Move Forward with Intention

Which of the 4Liberation Intentional Habits listed below, or create your own, will you put into action first to begin to heal your triggers and disrupt the fears inhibiting the best version of yourself? It takes approximately two months to create a habit. Once you establish a habit with one of the four intentions, consider applying another 4Liberation Habit.

Habit #1: Choose Gratitude

Reflecting on what you are grateful for is a transformative agent for healing. Choose to start your day with a show of gratitude to mark the blessing of another opportunity to express love to yourself and others. You are uniquely you, and making the decision to honor and celebrate who you are evolving into and what you aim to bring to fruition diffuses triggers. Starting a daily gratitude journal or even texting yourself daily one thing you are grateful for will help you find joy in small moments that make life beautiful.

Habit #2: Ground /Reset Yourself in Nature

Grounding prompts you to pause and shift to a safe space outside where you can hear the sounds of nature and experience the elements around you to center yourself. This can be as simple as opening your window in the morning and taking three cleansing breaths, taking a brief walk outside during your lunch break, or taking it to the next level by stepping outside of your residence, removing your shoes, and allowing the soles of your feet to connect your internal energy to the natural environment through grounding. If the outdoors isn't accessible at that moment, consider establishing elements of nature in your home or workspace by leveraging soothing sounds of nature, candles, diffusers, and or essential oils in rooms you frequent. The habit of grounding begins to disrupt internal chaos, mental anguish, and anxiety. When you are able to guide yourself to be still at times and at peace with your own silence, you are connected with your internal energy.

Habit #3: Proclaim Daily Positive Affirmations That Are Connected to Actionable Next Steps

The words you speak have power and play a major role in shaping the inner voice in your head. Visualize what you want your day to look like and how you want to show up in your life better than you did the previous day. Positive affirmations can fuel a day with intention through "I am" and "I will" statements. For instance, if you are anxious about an important work meeting or event on a particular day, recite affirmations such as, "I am enough and I will practice preparing for this meeting to help me better articulate my key points," or "I have valuable ideas to contribute and I will make it a point to express my ideas with my colleagues today." Start listening to yourself more and you will begin to see your ability to be more in tune and present in order to actively listen to others.

However, words alone are not enough. Liberation is rooted in action. Your affirmations are designed to establish mental models for change that provoke transformative actions. Consider your affirmations and commit to actualizing them. Be empowered to apply for a new job that is more aligned with your purpose, speak your truth to a family member, book a well-deserved vacation, or even check yourself into a rehabilitation center. Your liberation will only go as far as you drive it.

Habit #4: Enact Healthy Boundaries as Self-Care

Remove your people pleasing superhero cape, rescuing other's crown, and save-the-day pendant! Creating boundaries is healthy. When you want to improve your ability to maximize your day, it begins with managing your time with boundaries. Give yourself permission to decline invitations and minimize commitments. Setting boundaries still requires you to establish efficiencies such as creating an evening routine, even if you have children, so that you will have adequate time to spend with your family, but also independent time to decompress.

Similarly, enforcing boundaries with family, friends, and colleagues allows you to prioritize your personal wellness by choosing to do things such as taking leave from work to prioritize a day of relaxation, declining to host a holiday event at your home, or simply turning your phone on silent after eight o'clock in the evening. When you don't create space and time for you to care for yourself, you cannot model how you want others to treat you. Your self-care is the standard, and you deserve a standard of excellence.

chapter nine

Untethered by Activating "In Spite of" Energy

When I was a teenager, my father expressed that he wanted to go to seminary school and become a pastor. When he completed his studies, he began reaching out to people to invite them to his Sunday service. At that time, he wasn't able to secure a church building, so he held services in the basement of our 900 square-foot ranch-style home. Our pint-sized home looked as if it was inhaling and holding its breath, tight-lipped and congested with rental furniture and aged appliances. It was a humble house, but it was our home. Because we wanted to fully support my father with launching his church, our weeks were filled with making dozens of copies of flyers advertising the Sunday service and handing them out throughout our neighborhood and grocery stores.

Each Sunday, we waited with anticipation to see who would show. For a little over one year, we had one family join the Sunday service. I am eternally grateful to the Raby family for believing in my father's vision and trusting God to support him, even when the challenges of building a new church weighed heavily on them. Nonetheless, throughout each week, I heard my father's baritone African accent echoing through the upstairs floorboards as he practiced his message. My father repeated verses with darting inflections and bellowed out rhetorical questions as if the walls of the basement could attempt to respond back. He consistently gave me a stack of flyers week after week, which felt like trick-candles that wouldn't be extinguished. The flame ignited the hope that each recipient of a flyer would join our parishionless basement, but the reality of the candle wax dripped with despair with yet another Sunday with only the Raby family filling the seats. Being the rambunctious teenager I was, I sometimes wanted to refuse to hand out the flyers and tell my father that no one was coming. However, the determined look in my father's eyes gave me one of the most important lessons I still carry today. My father's light brown, almond shaped eyes filled with faith taught me to believe in myself, even when the optics told a different narrative. Each time he handed me a stack of flyers, his eyes said, "One day more people will come, and until then, I will continue to preach to my fullest potential."

I was, and still am, one of my father's, or should I say Reverend Jordan's, biggest supporters. He is truly committed to being a resource *and* a vessel for God to work through. Each service he facilitated with us and the Raby family, his eyes looked over the makeshift podium, made of garage sale shelving and cloth embellishments that my mother used to jazz up the podium. My father, Reverend Jordan, handed out the weekly bulletin announcements and offering plate with pride as if the empty chairs that gazed back at him communicated the promise of a future congregation.

My father led church in the basement of our home with pride, *in spite of* the muted choir that hadn't yet been formed, forcing him to sing praise and worship songs in tenor and soprano while we attempted to compliment the melodies. He led in the basement of our home with humility *in spite of* having to work two full-time jobs to support our family due to the lack of income provided by tithes and offerings from the *memberless* church. My father led in the basement in our home with liberation *in spite of* the bondage—lurking fears of the church not expanding, sending his vision to destinations never reached.

Living and leading with liberation calls on you're *in spite of* energy. The reflections you shared in the workbook were intended to help you unearth your 'in spite of energy' and spark the process of checking in on your bamboo roots. Take three deep cleansing breaths and state the following affirmations aloud as you take your new learning forward to shape the life and leadership posture that is uniquely yours. Recite the following Liberation Affirmations each day as you begin your journey. Even when your day is challenging, embrace your liberation *in spite of* being in the midst of a test. Your test will become your testimony!

Daily 4Liberation Affirmations

- I inhale light and love and exhale anxiety and negativity.
- I embrace peace and purpose and release self-doubt and judgement.
- I accept healing and forgiveness and disrupt bondage and self-harm.

- Self-care is my standard, not perfection.
- I am a leader and have the power to empower myself and others.
- I am a resource and a vessel.
- I am a disruptor of hate, bias, and judgement.
- I will live my life with intention and authenticity.
- I deserve self-care and self-love.
- I choose healthy habits, healthy REALationship, and healthy boundaries.
- Love, light, and liberation are my birthrights.

Thank you for being an integral part of *my* liberation. I pray that by sharing my journey and leadership best practices you are inspired to do the same. Together we are aligned to a better version of ourselves for the new era ahead. Congratulations for giving yourself permission to live and lead with liberation! Your new convictions will spark your purpose, peace, and passions for decades to come!

References

Simone, Nina, “Feeling Good.” I Put a Spell on You,” 1965

Simone, Nina, “I Wish I Knew How It Would Feel to Be Free.” Silk and Soul, 1967.

Warren, Rick, (2002). *The Purpose-Driven Life : What On Earth Am I Here For?* Grand Rapids, Michigan: Zondervan,

X, Malcolm, “Who Taught You to Hate Yourself.” Lost Angeles, California, 1962

About The Author

For over two decades, Leslie has served as an educator and leader, championing equity-centered learning for both students and teachers. She has remained committed to leading in urban school districts to ensure high quality, antiracist school experiences are the standard for all school communities, especially those that are often marginalized.

Leslie's passion for education started during her tenure as a National Board-Certified English Teacher and evolved into increasing her impact in subsequent roles as a District Master Educator, Assistant Principal, Principal-in-Residence, and district-wide Director of Leadership Development. Currently, Leslie serves as the Senior Project Director of Transforming Teaching, shaping what the role of teaching can look like in our nation's capital, the District of Columbia.

Leslie believes that living and leading liberation begins with interrogating biases, disrupting systemic barriers, and stepping into the power of being a change agent. As a proud mother of two children, Leslie stanchly advocates for whole child and whole adult success as the North Star for every school district and organization.

Contact

If you wish for Leslie Edwards to participate in workshops, interviews, writing, blogging, or speaking engagements, please send an email to:

LeslieEdwards@EdLeadership4Liberation.com

Learn more about the leadership services Leslie Edwards offers at www.EdLeadership4Liberation.com.

Individual, cohort, and staff development workshops can be customized to meet your liberation needs.